Secret Sauce
to
Goldilocks

Sonal Srivastava

Presentation by *BookLeaf Publishing*

Web: www.bookleafpub.com

E-mail: info@bookleafpub.com

ISBN: 9789363313613

First edition 2024

More Novels from Sonal Srivastava

Winning Your Demons - Answer To Your
Sorrows

The Yodha of Our Times - The Unsung Heroes
Of Today

The Real Reason Why - Journey of Two
Soulmates

Dedication Page

The

dedication

of this book

is split

in 9 ways;

to Parul;

to Dad;

to Mom;

to Nitin;

to Neetu Didi;

to Papa;

to Maa;

to Shreya;

to the BookLeaf Publishing House;

ACKNOWLEDGEMENT

YOU KNOW WHAT. However, you know all that your mind has perceived and wouldn't be very sure until you can be proved. This book unveils a recipe and the essence of winning and growth in life. The verses in this book reveal various secrets that could bring a life transformation in just 21 days!
Don't believe it? Try it and know your own way.

PREFACE

Excerpts in this book highlight how in 21 days
you can transform your habits and achieve all
that you have aspired to. You don't have to wait
till you struggle the most or use your smartness
to con someone to get all that you want.

All you need to do is, follow the small steps that
lead the way to transformation. With every poem
and practice, you begin seeing progress that was
somewhere stuck just in your thoughts or
tangled in your head. Enjoy this transformation
every bit for 21 days.

CONTENTS

27 Ribbons

27 ribbons,
Wrapped a pair of eyes;
Living in darkness,
Calling it life.
With each ribbon,
Unfolding a new sight;
Liberating from a truth,
That had worn a disguise.

Of these, 20 ribbons spoke of their hues;
7 other colors,
Defined a million truths.

The darkest one,
With a tinge of purple;
Was difficult to see,
At a mere glance.
It spoke of heights,
Of the spiritual roads;
That required no flight,
To reach the unknown divine.

The shade of blue,
Dispersed calmness,
Surrounding nature,
With peaceful bliss.

Green reflects the nature;
A law in defense.
Existing long before,
Human life had begun.
It flourished,
In the yellow sunrise,
In its brightness,
Aware of the intense guiding light;
Leading the growth of life on our planet.

From the yellow rising sun
Came through the sunset.
As the guiding light,
Powered its living legend;
Greeting the luminescence of the moon,
In its presence.

The white ribbon
Always laid the base.
Emerging in colors;
Taking different shapes.

From the orange shade,
Of a dimming sun,
A leading golden light emerged,
For all to see.
The light casted hue of bright red;
That left the sight,

In a delusion of self.
Yet, unless the ribbon
Remains tied,
None will know,
Of the real vision;
The stars and moons,
And what lies beyond the mind.

Collecting your Pieces

Kabir's Ultimate Den

In a dessert of over 20 thousand men,
Stood Kabir's store of grains and nuts;
Priced sufficiently well.

The barren land was the house of crew,
Some traveled to further lands while some had
no clue,
All they knew was Kabir's den,
His grains have always helped;
In all amends.
To reach his palace of ultimate grains,
There was a route to travel which wasn't plain.

On this path, many lost their towers,
Hazy blues and storms would shower;
It wasn't easy to reach the grains of life,
So it needed dedication and detached insights.
Though once they tasted the grains of life,
They would learn of divine skies.

Kabir had told them many times,
"To get a grain, show me the price."
In this regard, the route would decide;
If the traveler is wrong or right.

Millions tried to reach the grain-filled paradise;
But none could reach Kabir's sight.
One knew nothing;
Directionless,
And discovered Kabir's hidden den.

Just a Thought

One thought,
And the path is paved;
Whether you have taken the decisions,
Or travel on the road, persisting in similar ways.
Whether or not,
You have decided
To roll down your ball,
Like you do in a bowling game;
Whether or not,
You want to cuddle
In the blissful rains.
One thought,
And the path is paved.
It's engraved;
Deep into your,
Clever mind.
Looking at ease;
No matter the time.

So think as you do;
Mindfully,
Think like you do;
Positively,
If you can incorporate,
These seeds in your mind,
You will grow plants,
That would help you climb;
To your cloud of dreams,
That you mentally own;
And call it "Mine."

Your Missing Spot

Are you looking
In the right place?
What you're looking for,
Is well-placed.
In the depth of your soul,
You're searching for;
A fix in another mold.

Have you not
Been here before,
Oh, fella!
Have you not
Sold the gold?
A gold of your
Heart and mind;
Storing peacefulness,
and divine vibes.

If you wish,
To find more of
Your fix from the broken world,
Close your eyes and look deep within;
Identify what's causing you pain.

Wandering in Wonderland

Oh feather!
Where do you fly?
Take me with you;
In the sky so high.
I am certain,
I would restore.
All the rush,
My emotions have found,
No control;
I would soar,
Like colorful birds;
Liberated, though unheard.
Unchained in expectations,
Unchained without force,
Unchained from the pressure;
Higher designations would know.
No matter what it brings,
Oh, dear feather!
Hear me now,
Take me to a horizon
With peace and love above.

Waking dream

Must you not miss,
The sip of relief,
Amidst a deserted day of struggle.

Must you not keep,
Yourself on the feet;
Lest you forget the meaning of stable.

Must you not pamper,
The agony of the moon;
For it is just a passing fervor.

Must you not sip tea,
In the midst of a waking dream,
It may just lose its flavor.

Your one stop

Is this it?
Is this what I weigh?
Should this be,
The only conclusion to the game?
The loop of moon and sunlight,
Is this all to be called a life?
Must I not run,
And find a stop?
Before I begin,
To reach another spot.
Must this be the only,
One respite-earning to create;
a paradise.

Must I decide to take control,
Gradually, before the list overflows.
Must it be defined,
In my own thoughts;
Strengthening my self-control
Despite the odds.
I know one day,
As and when I rise,
I will see the sunshine,
Brighter in my life.

If not, small steps?

If not, small steps,
How far can you get?
How far?
How further?
Have you thought,
Of the route, you want to chart?
Would you be stuck,
In the hurdles of life—without yourself,
By your side?
And if you are complacent
In your mind
Of your state
Then, do you think,
It would lead you to the desired place;
Without the taste of efforts and sweat?

No win,
Hits differently in our minds;

Like the one we have journeyed,
For a long time.
From the beginning of the road,
Until the end.
Finding solutions;
To mend your ways.
All for the people,
And yourself.
With a million smiles brimming,
By the time of the win.

Without the attempt,
Do you think?
It would take you to your desired place?
How far and how much further;
Can you take yourself?
If you don't step up;
And handle the reins well?

Would it be really enough?
Would you finally take,
That one step?
Letting it loose
To cater to yourself?
If you don't,
You know, it's your loss!

None would know,
Of the hidden pearl you hold!

Unless you don't step back,
And take a turn to see—
A full 360 degrees of all that has been,
You won't be able to hear then,
Your life is full of melody within.

Find your Find

Sit and see;
The colors you want,
Think it through;
Before it's gone.
Think and see;
How you will make,
Your life brighter;
With its shade.

When you imagine,
The sight to be;
You will realize,
You're looking for your melody.

Call it a sunrise

Sugar,
Your daddy is running around;
Wake up before it has you bound.
Wake up to the light and sound.
Till when will you leave yourself;
On the ground?
Time is ticking;
Day and night,
In the moon and the sunlight;
Sugar, hurry!
It's about time.
Rise before they call it sunrise.

Foster your Passion

Foster, oh you must!
Not in the dust,
Not in the bubble of champagne,
Not in the activist campaigns
Foster, if you must,
Should it be then,
For yourself;
In the horizon,
Set up
Your dreams and passion,
For you to be able to,
Accomplish your own dares;
Dates that liberate in the
Darkest hours,
Chasing passion,

Regardless of the stars,
Foster, if you must,
Must it be in your glow,
Loving your passion,
No matter how slow.

Circle Again

Circles;
yet another one.
And of them all,
Don't we remember some?
Only some;
We do remember again,
For others wondering,
What we can't change.

So this morning,
I thought of changing the game;
Let the day throw curves,
Untamed.

Struggle;
I will, for the millionth time.
Since we have decided to call it life.
Cuddle I will,
Again, for the millionth time;
Despite the pricks
Disguised by the marching time.

Circle again,
I will, for another day.
Within my blanket of thoughts;
Cozy in my laze.

Prepare again,
I will, for the time;
To win the race,
When the power will be mine.

Your three pebbles

Three pebbles,
And you can cross a sea
How would you use them;
With stability?

Three pebbles,
No thoughts;
How would you cross,
The big sea, full of sharks.

Three pebbles,
That can float you,
Far enough,
To take you across,
From one shore to another.
Three pebbles,
One thought;
And you could,
Find yourself sitting in a world of dreams,
You have only just imagined.

The first pebble—
Would you try?
Step on it,
Or in the water, it flies?
Unless you don't

Set this piece right,
It would sink deep inside.

Strengthen your base
Each time.
Until you know,
You can easily stand firm.

Strengthen your mindset
To be disciplined,
Every time;
The laziness,
Knocks the door of your mind.

The second pebble,
Could be another step,
If you know exactly,
What is the depth;

With much understanding,
Of the drop,
You can create a base,
That's much more strong.

With much more determination,
In your mind,
Should you plan a strategy,
That can take you,
Where your dreams reside.

The third pebble,
Is a million-worth choice,
Use it wisely,
And proceed without a noise.

Should it be well-knitted;
In your thoughts,
The diligence it deserves,
Until you reach your goals.

Or must you not,
Combine the stock?
Make it a tool,
To fix in a spot.

A powerful tool,
That can disguise,
A leading light,
In the darkest night.

Let it float;
Until it stops,
Near the shallow,
Shore of your thoughts.

Must you not,
Follow the stones;
Must you let it,
Go on its own.

Stabilizing a base,
You have dreamt,
For so long.

Of the Mindset

No matter what she tried;
They repelled,
A million times.

Was it the lack,
Of her mind?
Or was it the emotions,
That was not right?

She tried and tried,
And finally cried;
Why would they not,
Appreciate her style?

And then a thought,
Rose in her mind;
Would it be fair,
To share what she liked,
With just another,
Pair of eyes?

She hesitated,
And took a step;
In the ocean of leaders,
Who knew of the best.
Her diligence held;
Her confident soul,
As she began to share,
Her work grew bold.

It was different;
Not wrong or right,
Just a thought,
That hadn't occurred in their minds.

Many rejected,
Many felt apprised;
Yet the majority wished,
To invest at a good price.
As they began,
Appreciating her work;
She knew it was something,
Her efforts deserved.

Often times,
The mind is right;
It's just the conflicts,
Living in clashing minds.
Minds that believe,
In retaining the old,
And of the thoughts,
That breathes on the new and bold.

Always remember,
Nothing is wrong or right.
Your boat will find you,
On a shore awaiting your sight.

Inner Spark of Power

One fine day,
There was a breakout.
And then,
Everything!
All possible existence;
Changed for good.
For a greater good;
That unfurled miracles.

Finding your Balance

What is Balance?

A misconception;
A misheard,
Misspoken,
Misunderstood perception.
Have you ever
Described to yourself
And noticed,
You are only narrating
The same song?
Balance defines,
Each of your own;
Mind, strength and your mental weather.
There's no ideal,
No particular known;
That would help you,
Get it together.
Practice you may,
Of what leaders have said;
A tell-tale
Can be a part of your narrative.
Learn from the experienced;
Make your own,
One only path to travel.

Stir Slow

Don't rush,
I know the day is crawling;
And the time might have you falling;
Don't rush.

Don't rush,
For the cake takes time to bake;
No matter what the stomach says,
Don't rush.

Don't rush,
It's a false alarm;
You have to proceed with calm.
Don't rush.

Don't rush,
For you will not know,
How much more,
You could have added to the glow.
Don't rush.

Don't rush,
Because if you do,
Time will still be ahead of you.
Only with patience,
Can you win this race.
The clock takes a circle,
To call it a day;
Don't rush.

Focus on the small growth,
Take time to let the plant explore;
The pattern that suits it right,
For growing in a direction,
You wouldn't have in mind.
Don't rush.

It's not easy to open a door.

One golden chance

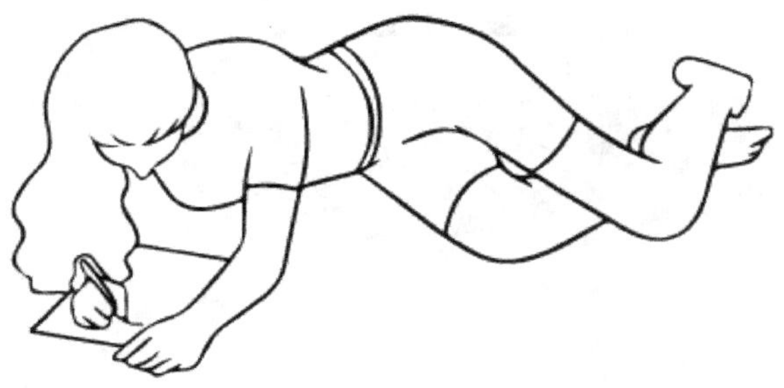

20 times I tried,
And there was only once,
Where I could find;
What it could be,
For it wasn't me,
Who tried and tried,
Perhaps even cried;
Wasn't it me?
Who had to see,
Success finds those
Who live the life,
Submerged in struggles,
Emerge in the shining light.

Food for Thought

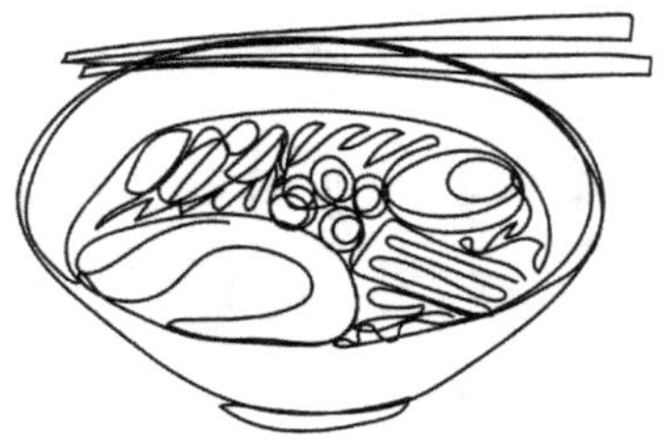

Circles;
How would you complete,
An eternity?
For there is something,
Beyond your set impossibilities.
In circles,
We fill our minds,
With coins, the Sun, the Moon—
Nearly all that for which,
We actually care.
No matter what time,
No matter when;
The pattern remains,
As you have ingrained,
Every time.

In a circle,
Just like you had designed,
A circle is—
A reflection of our minds.

A loop full of only hope,
A loop full of no direction,
Unless you navigate the rope.
A loop full of healthiness,
A loop full of motivational & creative sense,
A loop full of leadership,
Yet a loop full of ownership,
A loop full of just desires,
A loop full of passion & fire,
A loop full of golden glow,
A loop full of cold snow.

All we did,
Was only rhyme;
With the circles of heart,
Ruled by mind.
All we did,
Was only rhyme;
With the tug & pull,
Called your life.

Pick it up

Pick up;
If you haven't yet.
Pick up;
So you don't regret.
Pick it up;
It's just a broken piece.
Pick it up;
No, you're not a thief.
Pick it up;
For, if you won't,
Someone else will come and own.
Pick it up;
This is your call;
Pick it up;
You know, it's not worth the loss.
Pick it up;
You have been waiting for long.
Pick it up;
Before it's all gone.
Pick it up,
For your only vision.
Pick it up;
For your self-driven vision.
Pick it up;
You can make a miracle,
Shine in the air;

Like a sparkling star.
Pick it up;
A story is waiting,
For a character,
In its making.
Pick it up;
Don't let your power get lost,
In the whirlwind of life,
And all the chaos.
Pick it up!

Not enough

It's not enough;
It can never be.
No matter what,
Until you feel the relief.

It's not enough;
Until you see the shine,
In the details of a masterpiece,
Awaited by time.

It's not enough;
Till you strike the line.
That one imperfection,
That would make it right.

It's not enough;
Unless you're mesmerized.
By your own creation,
Any day or night.

It's not enough;
You can ask your mind.

When you know,
Something is missing;
Despite what seems right.

It's not enough;
But you can make it right,
Just think about it,
What sets it apart,
From the ocean of pride.

It's not enough;
Until it shines like the moon,
No matter what the weather,
It shines through and through.

It's not enough;
Until it sparkles in your eyes,
Just like the fairytales,
When the prince meets his bride.

It's not enough;
Until it makes you think,
What could it be,
That had you synced.

It's not enough;
To make you wonder,
Of the miracle,
You could stride;

To create a glory,
Only you could see
With closed eyes.

One Spark

Sea waves
Bring a peace to the mind;
Yet the uncertainty tickles
The wisdom of mind.

Every morning,
When I hold my flask
Pouring some hot tea
To a thoughtful glass.

A battle begins
In my thoughts
Of all that I did,
And all that I forgot.

Of the things
That stayed in my mind
The fire in me
Settles the rambling rhyme.

Let's go step by step;
It decides.
For you need to be mentally free,
Before you begin to write.

Write for a miracle;
It decides.
Words are not worth throwing,
Like melting ice.

In every blink,
Of my eyes,
My thoughts carve a story;
I call it life.

Every minute
You blink your wandering eyes;
Hoping for a miracle to appear in disguise.

Every second
When you breathe or sigh,
A thought has changed the perceptions of your
mind.

Every breath
When you solve a task,
Your brain develops a faith that builds and
basks.

Every faith,
Within your mind,
Tells you of the miracle you can make inside.

Every sunset,
Every sunrise,
Is writing the stories of your life.

Every meal,
That you feed on time,
Merges with the positive thoughts of mind.

Every struggle,
Pulls an inch;
Closer to the circle,
We often think we begin.

Earning Value

It's not a click of your fingers;
Neither is it a twitch of your eye.
It's not just your luck;
But beyond the favors of the universe and life.

To earn your value,
Every bit
Requires a disciplined mind.
To earn value,
And respect,
You must respect your own life.
Unless you don't set limits;
Life will let loose—untied.

Unless you lose;
You won't earn.
The deal wouldn't take,
A different turn!
Unless you realize,
What it is like;

Running a race,
You did not decide.

Would you know,
What it is like?
To stop and think;
What happened to your life?

Unless you lose yourself;
You don't realize,
The value of giving it everything;
Equally, every time.

The Certain

It's another day;
We have spent thinking.
What can we try
To bring in?

When 24 hours,
Seem like 25;
You know your day,
Will drag on till midnight.
When 24 hours;
Feel a bit tight,
The leader in you is thinking,
How to fight the difficulties of life.
To activate the yodha of your head;
You must let it think,
Proactively until you win life's simple bets.

It's certain;
To see another night,
As the moon gets dressed;
For its date night.

Yet again, we would only think,
Without realizing,
We need to learn how to begin.
When we start

To think at night,
We postpone our actions,
Until the morning light.

With the brightening clouds,
And a new sunlight,
We get busy;
With the daily knots.
By the evening,
When we realize
Another way to the only goal,
Emerges in our minds.

So which way,
Would you run?
The one you chose;
Or the one you found,
At the rising sun?

No matter what
Path you decide,
Remember, never let your ideas
Archive.

Settle Strong

Settle;
In the bright sunlight,
Feel the hesitance,
Of your complacency;
Questioning your thoughts—
Settle.

Brew your morning thoughts
As you get accustomed,
To the loving warmth,
Of the sun.

It may be harsh,
Despite the morning hours;
But you must settle.

Settle in the noise;
Distracted by the chirping birds.
Settle in the sound of
Droplets merging,
In a pool of water,
Growing by itself.

Settle;
No matter how long,
The tunnel of your day seems.

Settle;
Like a soft falling feather,
Moving slowly with grace;
And settling on the ground delicately.

There's no push;
There's no run.
There's no relief;
There's no pun.
There's no distance;
There's no shortcuts.

All there is:
Settle to be you.
Settle strong;
Like you always wanted to.

Endlessly

How hard,
Will this constant fight be?
How hard,
Can I live to be free?
My mind has broken;
So has the heart.
Life seems to venture,
Into an endless dark.
Will there be a light in the end?
There often is in such tunnels!
There is no pretense.
No room to lose hope.

All I can do is;
Keep it on the go.

Yet the light within me,
Guides my mind;
To a million possibilities.

Stairway to the only shore,
Where peace resides,
Without efforts.

Emerge

Watching Dawn

Sounds faded,
Like the disappearing bubbles,
Of coffee.
Words that wrote,
Another promise for tomorrow
Received another email header.
These words,
Watched the evening dawn.
The sky changing colors;
Blue, yellow, orange,
Submerging in blue clouds.
Sighing as they end the day;
That was created with effort.
These words,
Eventually drove happily home;
These words,

Wore another mood;
Lively yet calm, in their own world.

For the ones;
That stayed back to be strong.
A little more effort,
To be well-known;
The day had ended,
Before they could see.
Sounds had faded;
Before their last meal.
The miss of the day,
The miss of the night,
The miss of taste,
The miss of life,
Just for one,
Goal in mind.
Has not driven;
You up the sky.
Unless you don't press,
The brakes of your drive;
The car will crash,
In the speed and light.
It will then,
Leave you alone;
Injured and emotionally torn.

By the time,
You would realize,

What you have missed,
In your life.
Your efforts must be multiplied;
to calm the storm.
Bring the balance,
While you stay strong.

It isn't impossible;
There is a bright light.
The vision of which,
Is visible
Only when you have,
Made your time right!

Would you not,
Want to hold the stick straight?
Walk effortlessly,
Without any fear?
Begin to calm,
Your beating heart.
Conquer your fears that would,
Leave you only alone and starved.

Legend of rice grains

At times,
The taste of rice
Is not so apparent,
Under the rhetoric muses,
Of flavors and added;
Vegetables and salts,
We then name it
Identified within a different lot.

Have you ever then,
Put a thought;
Why is rice so famous,
When there's a variety of whatnot?

The unspoken legendary,
Has learnt to imbibe;
A story of a thousand souls,
No matter the life.

The unspoken grain,
Has made a legend.
By being the core,
Of any cuisine;
Prepared and given.

The unspoken rice,
Only mingled with spice;
Glittered in a million, several skies.

And all that we can,
Learn and realize;
The work done in silence,
Speaks a million times
Than the thousand flavorsome,
Promises of a sort.

Until you get,
To the main plot.
A thousand words,
Remain unrhymed,
Unless they embody;
A different style.

Must you create,
The unspoken thought;
That can spark a miracle,
In a million stocks.

Must you add,
The essential style;
That can embody all flavors,
And still stand as itself;
No matter the time.

One Decision Away

Now that you've decided,
To make your efforts shine,
I'm sure,
You'll make it
All the way,
Until it's time.

Now that you've decided,
To let yourself shine;
Make your work sparkle,
Like a billion diamonds,
In the sky.

Now that you've decided,
To make it all worthwhile;

Like mesmerizing landscapes,
Hanging on the wall.

Now that you've decided,
To set it right;
With all the success in life,
Until you rise.

Now that you've decided,
To make it one;
This is the only opportunity,
You could ever earn.

Now that you've decided,
To make it worth;
Make sure it stands out,
In this living earth.

Now that you've decided,
To make the effort;
Take all your strength,
And give it rhythm.

Now that you've decided,
This is the time;
You will no matter what,
Make it fly a thousand skies.
Now that you've decided,
To fill your pot;

With progressive vibes;
And much more of what you thought.

Now that you've decided,
To take it out;
Make it the most beautiful,
One could ever see in the crowd.

Now that you've decided,
This is the time;
Make it worth it,
Until you leave everyone mesmerized.

Now that you've decided,
To mine the coal;
Make it sparkle,
Like a living soul.

Now that you've decided,
To give it all your strength;
Make it powerful,
Like none can comprehend.

Now that you've decided,
To crack that goal;
Build the stairs,
And not a hole.

Now that you've decided,
To make the stairs;
Ensure they're smooth enough,
To let no one else dare;
Climb the steps,
That you have prepared.

No one deserves,
Your efforts and applause.

Now that you've decided,
To make it right;
Mindfully craft,
Your actions besides
Marking a beautiful,
Golden line.

Now that you've decided,
To make it whole.
Ensure it is;
Attempted by your very soul,
And you could own;
The Goldilocks alone.

Taking Flight

Don't chase the butterfly;
You have found yourself,
In the alleys of undefined mind.

In its thoughts,
It has taken you on several flights,
Attempted to set yourself
On a false pride.

And maybe others feel
That's all right!
But when you question yourself,
Do you find yourself right?

Imagine if you claimed
Yourself to be that high,
Wouldn't the reality,
Feel more bright?

Why live a dilution?
When you can transform,
Small illusions?

Set your thoughts,
To align;
With the multiple goals,
That are awaiting
To create a legend,
A history; or a remarkable story.

An objective
Just for you,
So you can reach,
Your dreams,
One after another.

For none
Other than you to shine;
For if you wouldn't,
The magical water,
Will evaporate.

For if you don't
Then who will unlock
The vision to a new world,
Hidden under the shades
Of a passion that gave,
Life to some

Running on a road of
Burning stones.

For if not for you, sugar;
Would the world glitter
Or logically operate?

If this isn't your calling;
May you run.
To a lost island,
In the burning sun.
And then realize,
What you left behind;
To chase it back,
Till you explore it well and taste the success.
Hiding beneath your shoulders,
Full of responsibilities.

Sight of mind

It's all in the state of mind;
A pot full of,
several sights.

And he who holds the muse,
Has the strength to bring,
Delightful hues.

No matter the dust,
No matter the storm
He would chop the woods,
To keep his house warm.

Little would slip,
In the sight of mind;
To let his motivation,
Anchor the mind.

He knows well;
And she does too,
Of the oneness,
That eventually grows.

He knows exactly,
Where to stop.
Must the water not,
Splash out of the pot.

She knows which,
Spices are just right;
To bring the flavor,
That life wishes to try.

She knows well;
With the intensity of heat,
Would here soup,
Become a meal.

He and she,
Walk the same path;
Hoping to live a life,
Their minds would craft.

And have they thought,
Thought it right?
Is following the steps of leads,
The only sight?

Third Attempt

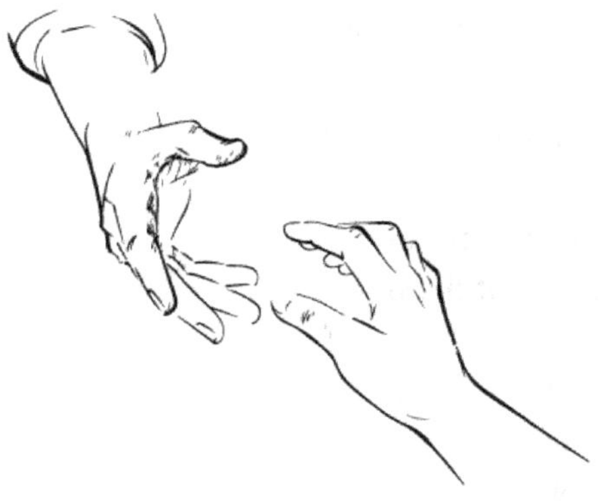

In the third attempt,
I knew it all.
Beans spilled a secret,
That I hadn't known.

In the third attempt,
When I achieved all that I could;
I knew the demons,
Were stronger than before.

In the third attempt,
Which was not the last;
I recognized the blind spots;
That would dance on the craft.

In the third attempt,
That I would embrace,
I understood the true value,
Of what's called gold.

In the third attempt;
And many more,
I know that something new,
Will replace the old.

In the third attempt,
I lost myself;
To regain my peace,
And my strength.

Of Your Skyline

Try;
Rise high,
In your own mind,
Then make an attempt,
To touch the sky.
Fly you can,
Without an airplane;
Once you have,
Strategized your ideas and plans.
No idea is small in life,
All you need is,
A strong mind.
Fly again,
Even after failed attempts;
Not like boiling milk,
But like the growing trees and plants,
Slow and small,

May be your steps.
But progress would wait,
At every turn.
Applaud yourself;
No matter what loss and win.
Applaud yourself;
For having taken a spin.
The spin often takes a turn;
Pauses before,
It can start anew.
Settle in the realm,
That you know well.
Shine;
Brighter than you could have felt.
Shine;
From your only core,
Without any struggles.
And peace restored.
Shine;
It's your time.
Shine;
The sun is waiting,
For your rise.

Your Secret Power

It takes power,
To make a change;
Live a dream,
And dare to wake.

It would be foolish a thought;
To stand and stare,
Watch opportunities pass by,
Without a care.

More foolish than the thought,
Is to make a prayer;
To avail a chance,
Only to make it there.

Opportunities aren't availed,
Or vanish into the air;
Victory comes when you create them,
In situations so rare.

Unleashing the Power

It's a power
That you ought to tap
It's a power
To which only you can attach.
It's a power
That can create your lucky time.
It's a power
That's supremely divine.
It's a power
That can beam the shine,
Shine that sets you apart from the crowd.
No matter the work,
Your efforts always count.
It's a power
That, if left untapped,
In your mind
You wouldn't realize,
Its presence at your disposal—

Anytime!
It's a power
That will show you,
The flavors of success
Don't come at just a sight,
But at a great price.